Views From My Life's Window

Savia Gracias Sanches

Presentation by *BookLeaf Publishing*

Web: www.bookleafpub.com

E-mail: info@bookleafpub.com

ISBN: 9789357749459

First edition 2023

Dedicated to

my darling husband Cristo

who always supports me and encourages me in
the most loving way

&

my beautiful children Judah, Cheruba and
Gianna

who are always inspiring me with their love and
affection for me

PREFACE

Writing poems always came naturally to me. My poems are linked to glimpses of my life and my own reflection on them. Without the various ups and downs, life wouldn't be like a rainbow. I believe that every situation in life is a lesson in its institution. And so, everything flows into the other. Thus, it is befitting to write poetry as poetry flows too. It is just so that one can connect various moments with a play of words, rhyme and pause to express one's feelings, one's life lessons, advice and struggles. This book is an opportunity for me to paint my life into the abstracts of poetry, some subtly, some loudly.

Parents, Not Choice

You did not choose me,
No, I chose you says the Lord.
I did not choose my parents
But neither did they me.

I was loved
I was pretty
I was girl
I was his
I was hers
Was I ever theirs?

Yet I wondered
I did not choose them nor
They did me
Why?

I wondered
I cried to my pillow -
Put me to sleep
I cried to the ground -
Swallow me up

Was marriage always a painful affair?
Did true love always lead to despair?

Was doubt always the background to loyal
spouse?
Were cries always the music heard in a good
house?

When will this end, O God when?
I learnt to pray
Give me the strength, O God, then
The courage to stay
The flower of acceptance bloom
 My parents reach not doom
....
For they did not choose me
Nor I them
But You chose us
Not us You.

An Ode to my Mother

Strange to a familiar land
You came
You saw
You conquered

Brave-faced
Bronze-armed
Big-hearted
Beauty beaming aura

Ma, you were
Still are
Will be
Source of my courage
Strength and
Song

Mother, you bore us
Like father, you raised us
As friend, you guided us
As teacher, you edified us

Through storm and strife
While struggles were rife
Even at the point of a knife
Battered wife

Your resilient smile
Probably was our forte
Our giggles and laughter
Enough reason for your mirth

Many a dead end
Did your roads bring
But you just turned around
Walked with swing

Your avatars were a-changing
Sometimes shielding her children, a fortress
Sometimes guarding her cubs, a lioness
Other times a candle, spent in her burning

Rainbows you looked for
The rain hardly stopped
Relenting the skies cleared
A bright, new sun looked out

Your light keep on shining
May happiness be your partner dining
Reign on,
Ma, reign on!

Sea of Innocence

5

As a baby
I remember
Showers of love
In the garden of innocence
Adam and Eve
Toiled hard
Sweat of the brow
Provided for

In the lap of love
I sat gurgling
Memories flooding
The river of my soul
Over rocky mountains
Have I come
To meet my life's sea
So have I come to be

Flowing
Crashing
Laughing in high tide
Ebbing away in low tide
Memories like footprints
In the sands of my life's time
Some effaced

Some re-lived
Some tossed away
Like algae

I stand
Like a pillar of salt
That looks ahead
Remembering always
The sea that formed me
So have I come to be

Blooming flower of youth

As a flower blooms
I bloomed
Unfurled my pretty petals
To the sound of screeching kettles

As I looked up
I saw the blue
Cheerful sky
Unheard was my cry

How beautiful the world seemed suddenly!
Hope surged suddenly!
Faith jumped suddenly!
While a pinprick nagged me achingly

I looked on
As a flower does
To beholders
In whose eye beauty was
Maybe I would be
Maybe I would see
Life, love, glee

I want to be

I beheld the singer of pop
With eyes like corn…popped
I hearkened to the radio jockey
With ears cocked while having my coffee

I fancied being a crooner
Who would pop the charts one day
I remember practicing before the mirror
Dancing wanton sway

I fancied being a pancake turner
One day I'd be flooded with emails
From fans who my voice did garner
Leaving radio trails

I wanted to reach the stars
The star I wanted to be
I wanted to touch the skies
The sky wanted to be me

Smitten

That was the age
Of stars and moons
Spinning around me
It was an astronomy
Sorta new

Biology too
Lay defeated
Who could explain
Pulsing veins
A heart
That came to a screeching halt

Reverie was the world
I lived in
Could hardly tell
The difference
Between dream
And a real-life sequence

Suddenly aware
Felt the stare
Suddenly woman
Life was lemon
A loving face flashed
In my mind unabashed

My heart it fluttered
Like a garden watered
Drenched in love
Rose like a dove
Sank in quick sand
Rose again
Sank again
Pause…pause...pause

My Alpha and my Omega

You formed me in my mother's womb
Knit my insides,
My sinews, my flesh, my womb
You held together in Your sight!

Out in the world You brought me forth
Like a lamb among the pack of wolves
Meek and shy, both
Yet wise in a world of fools

For you I have made myself a fool
After all, I found my treasure
In Your hands, I am just a tool
In Your presence, I find utmost pleasure

The louder the noise, the harder
It is to hear You,
Silence is golden, the better
It is to be near You.

Truly I live on borrowed time
If not for You, not worth a dime
Your ransom for me was not a loss
I now am lover of Your cross

In the end, all stories must come to an end
I confess, in You I found my true friend
Glory I do not seek, but a happy death
When You shall take back from me your breath

The Breath of God

You had planned my life from the beginning of the
universe
The length, the breadth, for better or for worse
I was born but a mere clay pot in the Potter's hands
His Breath made me human, I am His brand

O Breath of God, who so gently blow
Like a wind you come into the upper room
Transforming into love
The hearts set on doom

O Breath of God, you set alight
My heart with a flame, so warm and bright
Like a pillar of fire
Walking with me in the long dark night

O Breath of God, you flow like a river
Shaping hardened rocks by day
You cut through and through like a double-edged
sword
Softer still, You make a way

The hearts of wise men are set on you
The fools they do not know you
More precious than incense, myrrh or gold
The Breath of God, no price to be told

Learning to Love

Like a gazelle, swift-footed
You came into my life
Before I was swept off my feet by distant winds
You swept off the ground 'neath my eyes

Your simplicity, love and affection
Were always more than a distraction
Your frankness, open-heartedness
Won me over, you are genius

My love, I learned to love
When your hand fitted mine like a glove
Above, in the skies above
My heart learned to soar like a dove

The Next Wonder of the World

Your love is like smoke
Which fills a room
One knows not how it sets foot there
Sitting on my lap, caressing my hair

Your love is like that invisible string
That pulls at my heart, ting-ting-ting
Even when you are out of my sight
Tugs at my heart, in the wind like a kite

Sometimes I wonder what I'm made of
I say I'm a tough gal
Wonder! As soon as I have you seen
My knees become jelly beans

My darling, how your love has me transformed
My view of the world have you reformed
I have become now the next wonder of the world
Wife, mother, business-woman, cook –
everything, all at once unfurled!

Adam's Rib

As I sit by the gurgling stream
Painted by the sky in bright pink
On a tuft of green grass
I slowly catch a wink

It is dusk, or is it dawn?
I see a horse, its rider swift
Before me he stood, suddenly
My lips he kissed

It was like a sleep-inducing potion
His eyes burning amber
I sank into deep slumber
In his arms asunder

When I awoke, I was still
Looking into his kind eyes
My surroundings I hardly noticed
The new world around me spun
Without wind, without sun

Even if he asked me to be his
I was already, without question
I felt like a newly created being

As if his heart was stirring inside me instead of
mine

Oh! I slipped in and out of darkness and light
I felt his rib cage
His rib I just be might
Coz his rib seemed to be amiss
Instead, I fit in that same crevice

Two hearts, One seal

Formed like an infinity ring
Two hearts and lives joined together
It isn't merely a love-sick feeling
But two beings entwined, tethered together

Sacrifice and forbearance afoot
Humility and forgiveness take root
The more 'I' disappear
The stronger 'we' become

Hand in hand as we walk
Our hearts start to talk
Bridges form over rivers and streams
Through stormy clouds shine heavenly beams

The one incomplete without the other
One is the better half of the other
Two hearts one seal
Forever love is real

Motherhood

How motherhood is born
From the loins of two
Beauty created by the fingers of God
In the inmost recesses
Suddenly the hardened heart
Melts down
Holding in inexperienced hands
Even after cruel labour
Maternal love to savour
Hail thee, O Motherhood!
Thou art divine
Through you God's love
On humanity shines!

Mom-e-sis

Heaven rejoiced
Earth resounded
Your family partied
When you were born
My children you are the curve of my smile
The reason for me to go the mile
Your first step made mine so many
I reached the corners of the earth to hold you
In my arms, a gift
In my heart, racing thoughts
Excitement rose
Flowers deluge
Unknown seams
My forever dreams
Took flight
I learned to learn
Loved to love
Your baby breath
Your discovering hands
Your baby babble
You were for me my bundle
Of joy
Joyful noise
Growing bubble
Bursting me

Metamorphosis
Mom-e-sis
Me and myself
Forever gone
When you were born

To my children, Pearls and Diamonds

Some parting words I'd like to say
They may seem black and gray
Even so, the most precious pearls and diamonds
dug

Honesty and hard work are like siblings
Ignore them not, they'll be
The ladder you need to climb

Smile at the new day
She'll send cheerfulness your way
Even in moments that hurt

Good friends treat with care
They are a find so rare
While enemies are a hurting handful
Beware! Your Facebook friends could be the
hateful handful
Good friendship is really so rare

Most of all be grateful
Follow not money and
It will follow you like a bunny
Be grateful, contentment is a happiness rule
While resentment is found in the heart of fools

To my Brothers, my Friends

Gratitude in my heart
For the way you play your part.
Life would be incomplete
Without brothers so sweet.
Such is a gift of brothers
A gift so rare.
To me as friends
Who are always there.
With you, childhood passed like a dream
The laughter and games we played
Still vivid, still real
Helping each other stand tall
Whenever we fall.
May God speed you
His angels guard you.

Gold and Pearl

As gold is purified in fire
So have I walked
Through fire and mire
For if I must be gold, then I must burn
And so have I been molten

My life is like an oyster
A speck of dust
Becomes pearl
So for me all struggles change for my good
All dust becomes pearl

Are you passing through fire?
Humiliated, scorned
Is a dust storm blowing in your life now?
Blamed, forsaken
Remember then, all things will turn for your
good
You are gold, you are pearl

Did I love?

I walked into a garden
Where the plants were as big as trees
The ants were like knights and horsemen
Armored up against the breeze
The busy dragonflies flitted around
Like busy drones
While the queen bees
Sat in their thrones
Awestruck me, open-mouthed me!
I exclaimed "This must be the Kingdom of
Awe."

As I continued strolling
I came upon a field of lilies
Butterfly girls were singing like sillies.
I chuckled at the colourful sight
Today the sun too was shining bright
Suddenly I came upon a wise old snail
Sliding along with a pail
He looked at me with observant eyes
That only made him look more wise

"Wanderer dear," he said to me
"What on earth are you looking for?"
"To belong," I replied

"By the looks of you,
You certainly don't look like you belong here,
child.
For to belong, you must love"
Then, my whole life flashed before me
The gardens and forests I had pillaged and burnt
Made lightning pictures in my head
"Do I belong here in this paradise?
Did I love? Did I …? Did I…?"

Pain

27

Pain is a part of life
Life partners with pain
Not the matter of
Whether you are sane
Or insane
Pain follows you
Like your shadow
Even in the beautiful meadow
Shine or rain
Following you is pain

Humility

Who said that
The grain of wheat
That fell to the ground
Remained there to rot and die?
Yes. It died
But just as it did
New life sprang up from the ground.

My friend dear
Did you fall?
Be not ashamed
This is humility's call
Pride is the mountain
That comes crashing
Down
Heed you my friend
The meek call of humility

Do you feel dead?
Do you feel trampled?
Scorned? Derailed?
Know you now
You will spring
Up with new life
Like the wheat grain

Humbled to the ground
Rising up.

Stay there, resolve
To never befriend
Such pride.
For humility is our power
Giving new life
Erecting pillars
Of strength
Resurrecting what's dead
As a newborn.

Happy death

Magnificent bungalows
Picturesque gardens
Velvet ensembles
Gluttonous buffets
Vain birthdays
High life
Deathly pride
Puffy talk
All wreak of the stink of Death
As a book comes to an end
Your life must end in a Happy death
Your start of your happy ever-after.
So pile up
Good works,
Good words
Humbleness
And prayer
So you may lie on them
On that last page
Of your life's book
Peaceful
Entering your ever after
Blissful, joyful.